No. LXXII.

THE MINOR DRAMA

LOVE AND MURDER:

FARCE, IN ONE ACT.

BY JOHN BROUGHAM.

TO WHICH ARE ADDED,

A Description of the Costume—Cast of the Characters—Entrances and Exits—Relative Positions of the Performers on the Stage, and the whole of the Stage Business.

With Cast of Characters, Stage Business, Costumes, Relative Positions, etc. etc

AS PERFORMED AT THE NEW YORK THEATRES.

NEW YORK:
SAMUEL FRENCH & SON,
PUBLISHERS,
38 East 14th St., Union Square.

LONDON:
Samuel French
PUBLISHER,
89 STRAND.

No Plays Exchanged or Sent on Approval.

INTERNATIONAL DESCRIPTIVE CATALOGUE OF PLAYS, AND DRAMATIC WORKS,

With a Descriptive List of Amateur Plays and Articles.

CONTENTS.

ALL MAILABLE ARTICLES IN THIS CATALOGUE SENT POST FREE.

In ordering and remitting by Mail always send Post Office Orders if possible.

POSTAGE STAMPS TAKEN IN PAYMENT.

NEW YORK:	LONDON:
SAMUEL FRENCH & SON,	SAMUEL FRENCH,
PUBLISHERS,	PUBLISHER,
38 E. 14th St., Union Square.	89, STRAND.

Payment MUST accompany each Order.

A Catalogue with above Contents Sent Free.

☞ Those who receive extra Catalogues, kindly hand them to Friends.

FRENCH'S

AMERICAN DRAMA.

The Acting Edition.

No. LXXII.

LOVE AND MURDER:

A

FARCE, IN ONE ACT.

BY JOHN BROUGHAM

TO WHICH ARE ADDED,

A Description of the Costume—Cast of the Characters—Entrances and Exits—Relative Positions of the Performers on the Stage, and the whole of the Stage Business.

AS PERFORMED AT THE NEW YORK THEATRES.

NEW YORK
Samuel French & Son,
PUBLISHERS,
No. 122 Nassau Street.

LONDON.
Samuel French,
PUBLISHER.
89 STRAND.

Cast of the Characters.—Love and Murder.

	Wallack's Theatre
Don Manuel	Mr. Reynolds.
Don Garcia	" Lyster.
Don Andrez	" Shirley.
Mickey Magra	" Brougham.
Anita	Mrs Stevens.
Isabella	Miss Fanny Dean
Ninetta	Mrs. Brougham.

LOVE AND MURDER.

SCENE.—*A Spanish Interior, enclosed all round—Garden seen beyond through windows—trellis-work, with vines, on* L. H., *in corridor.*

Enter ANITA, C.

Anita. Signor jealous pate is gone at last; now, to release my poor imprisoned sister. Isabella! you may come forth.

Enter ISABELLA, R. D. 2 E.

Isabel. My dear Anita, I dislike more than ever this perpetual game of hide and seek. I fear that some great annoyance to you will grow out of it.

Anita. Nonsense, my dear. Lewis is gone for the day—you know how absorbing his business is; he never by any chance returns until evening; it's hard, indeed, if I cannot have the society of my own sister: to tell you the truth, I am getting heartily tired of his absurd jealousies and caprices, and I don't care how soon an explanation may take place.

Isabel. Why has he such an objection to my being here?

Anita. It ain't you, love, that he objects to, but the whole female race: it was as much as I could do to retain Ninetta, my favorite but somewhat familiar waiting-woman. What do you think he says—the libeller—that women are never as pleasantly employed (to themselves) as when they are plotting mischief; now you know that's not the case. [*a guitar heard.*, U. E. L.] Do you not, Bel. Why, what's the matter, dear? you are blushing like a provence rose. Who is the musician?

Isabel. Don't go, dearest, it's nobody, only a street musician—some poor wandering mendicant.

Anita. Indeed, a most elegant street musician, a very distinguished-looking mendicant. Oh, sister, not to tell me of this!

Isabel. Who could have supposed he would be so foolish—so audacious—so wicked—to run such a risk.

Anita. Ah, you've caught the universal contagion, I see. Shall we have the street musician in?

Isabel. Not for the world, it would be so rash—so wrong—so imprudent. Do tell him to go away, then, dear. Ah, not yet, I mean, I don't wish him to be positively insulted, you know—common courtesy demands that much consideration.

Costume.—Love and Murder.

MANUEL.—Black frock coat, pantaloons, and Hessian boots.

GARCIA.—Spanish officer's uniform.

ANDREA.—Dark morning suit, large cloak, and sombrero.

MICKEY MAGRA.—Blue faded uniform coat, gray trowsers, and Spanish gaiters ; hat and scarf.

ISABELLA, }
ANITA. } Spanish walking dresses, high combs, and black veils.

NINETTA.—Scarlet dress with black body.

STAGE DIRECTIONS.

EXITS AND ENTRANCES.

L. means *First Entrance, Left.* R. *First Entrance, Right.* S. E. L. *Second Entrance, Left.* S. E. R. *Second Entrance, Right.* U. E. L. *Upper Entrance, Left.* U. E. R. *Upper Entrance, Right.* C. *Centre.* L. C. *Left of Centre.* R. C. *Right of Centre.* T. E. L. *Third Entrance, Left.* T. E. R. *Third Entrance, Right.* C. D. *Centre Door.* D. R. *Door Right.* D. L. *Door Left.* U. D. L. *Upper Door, Left.* U. D. R. *Upper Door, Right.*

*** *The Reader is supposed to be on the Stage, facing the Audience*

Anita. Certainly, my dear, you are quite right, he shall not be insulted. [*rings bell.*]

Enter NINETTA, R. 2 E.

You were wonderfully near the door, Ninetta.

Ninetta. Yes, ma'm, I was, that's the truth ; fact is, I forget exactly what the fact is, ma'm, but I was going to tell you something very particular.

Anita. Indeed ! Well, that may be so ; but remember one thing, Ninetta, you and I will have a serious quarrel if I find you using your ears at undue times.

Ninetta. Ears ! law, my lady, you ought to know that my ears wouldn't listen to anything they oughtn't to hear, if I was ever so inclined : it's perfectly wonderful how deaf they can be on occasions.

Anita. That's right, keep them so ; be discreet, and you shall not lose by it.

Ninetta. Ho, ho ! I'm getting into request at last.

Isabel. Don't you think, sister, that it is rather discourteous to keep a gen—I mean a musician—waiting ?

Anita. The height of rudeness. Pardon me, dear. Ninetta go and acquaint yonder musician, that we should like to hear a specimen of his ability a little closer.

Ninetta. Yes, ma'am. Musician, ha ! ha ! This looks as if it were going to pay. [*Exit,* C. L.

Anita. I suppose I had better find some employment elsewhere, eh, sister.

Isabel. What for, I should like to know ? Surely you can't think. There, don't look at me in that way : yes, you may. Isn't he a charming fellow ?

Anita. Of course he is—I'll take your word for it. You forget—I don't know the street mendicant.

Isabel. For shame, sister, to strike a fallen foe !

Anita. He comes. Now, pray remember, that on those occasions time flies with singular rapidity. When may I interrupt you ?

Isabel. When you please—in a few minutes.

Anita. About an hour, I suppose.

Isabel. Oh, sister, we should hardly have time to say, how do you do, to each other in an hour.

Anita. Ah, well, I won't intrude at all.

Isabel. Won't you, that's better still ; how kind of you.

[*Exit,* ANITA, R. C.

Enter NINETTA.

My lady, the musician. [*Enter* ANDREA—*they salute formally.*

Ninetta. If his notes ring as sweetly as his golden pieces, he's the very prince of tweedledums. [*Exit,* R. C.

Andrea. My own dear Isabella, I have dared to break the restriction you enjoined upon me, once more, although last evening you told me how suspicious Senor Manuel was ; but surely there can come no ultimate harm now, when we are pledged to bear each other's future fortune

Isabe.. Were he like other men, I should not fear, but he is so rash, so hasty, and so blindly jealous, that a vague apprehension encircles me while you remain : it was by a miracle that we escaped his notice last night when we parted.

Enter NINETTA, R. C.

Ninetta. Beg pardon, ma'm, for interrupting you, but I don't know if it's of any consequence; however, thinking it might, there's no knowing; I thought I'd just step in to let you know, as it's best, I think, to be on the safe side, if possible, that my master is coming up the walk.

Isabel. I knew there was great risk—great danger.

Ninetta. It doesn't matter much, ma'm, does it?

Isabel. Everything, Ninetta, everything. Can you not get Senor Andrea away?

Ninetta. So, so—the twangler's a senor is he—I thought as much. Don't know what on earth to do with him, ma'm. [ANDREA *gives money.*] Let me see. [*more money.*

Andrea. Let this quicken your understanding.

Ninetta. Now, don't interrupt me in such an unprincipled manner, and at such a critical crisis—there's no time for deliberation—step into this room, it's the housekeeper's—he never goes there; when the coast is clear, I shall return and let you out.

Andrea. Dearest Isabella.

Ninetta. Oh! there's no time for that sort of nonsense: in with you—that's it. [*puts* ANDREA *into closet.*]

Isabel. Not a syllable, Ninetta, for your life.

Ninetta. What do you take me for? Put a sudden stop to the first delightful dilemma I've had the pleasure to be mixed up in for such a heap of centuries. Away with you into my misseses' boudoir—that's sacred yet, [*exit* ISABELLA, L. 2 E.] he's coming, and somebody with him—so much the better. [*pretends to dust the things, and is going off as* MANUEL *and* GARCIA *enter*, R. C.]

Manuel. Is this the time of day you dust the furniture?

Ninetta. Any time that it wants it, sir. Well, I'm sure—teach me my business. [*Exit*, R. C.

Manuel. Ah! they are all in league together—of that there can be little doubt. Where have they hidden that villain? Most likely here; he could not have escaped without my notice: he is here! [*locks door*, R. 2 E.] Thou'rt caged, now, thou subtle soul-slayer. Answer me, Garcia; are you now astonished that I should make so deadly a resolve?

Garcia. Still there is a bare possibility that you may be in error. I entreat you to pause before you proceed upon a determination so fearful.

Manuel. No, no; I cannot be deceived. Last night I saw my wife. Oh! that I should live to name her with such a thrill of indignation. I saw her parting from this vile seducer. I wonder what withheld me from dealing retribution on the instant? Did I need further proof? I have it now; enough to steel my heart against all pity. He must die;

nor shall I sully my hands with his dishonored blood. Have you seen the bravo?

Garcia. My great friendship for you forced my better nature to yield. I have seen him.

Manuel. And will he undertake this matter?

Garcia. That, or any other, for a sufficient recompense, but still I counsel you to delay your purpose.

Manuel. Garcia, it is the greatest love that, checked or desecrated, turns to bitterest hate. Say no more—my mind's made up—his life only can atone in part for this blot upon my house's honor.

Garcia. A few moments' reflection only. Walk with me in the garden: remember, vengeance is not always justice, even when portioned out by law itself.

Manuel. Justice and vengeance are alike in this. What! must I not stay the machinations of the secret foe, who fain would rob me of domestic joy? Come, the air will cool my fevered blood, while we await this messenger of death? but the stab, that lets out his base life, will be but nothing to the soul-pang I am doomed to feel henceforward.

[*Exeunt into garden*, L. C.

Enter NINETTA, *cautiously*, R. C.

Ninetta. Now to liberate our trapped musician. A few more pieces in my purse, or I mistake me—the saints, how's this! door locked: ho! within there!

Andrea. [*within.*] May I come forth, Ninetta.

Ninetta. That you may not, Senor, and for the best of all possible reasons, you cannot—the door is locked.

Andrea. And Manuel locked it—what is best to be done?

Ninetta. Why you must be content to remain until I find a key.

Andrea. Hist, Ninetta, you must inform my brother Leon; tell him to hurry here, this jealous fool may, in his rashness, do some mischief else.

Ninetta. It shall be done, Senor, at once: I'll go myself; there's no knowing what may happen. [MICKEY MAGRA *sings outside.* Oh, good gracious! if I didn't forget all about that, I mean him; it's my new sweetheart—the green islander. I just hinted to him Senor Manuel would be out all day, and he's had the impudence, I suppose, to take it for an invitation. He's a nice-looking fellow, though he *is* my intended. I wish he was anything but a butcher; ugh! it's a terrible trade, but profitable however, and that goes a great way in the choice of a husband.

Enter MICKEY, R. C.

Mickey. Ah, my deludin Andelusian, if it isn't like shaking hands with the stars to look into your purty pair of Spanish eyes. I'm a Hottentot!—look at me; havn't I dressed myself up in the national costume to please you? though I must say it's rather an inconvenient hot weather uniform.

Ninetta. I'm obliged to you for the proof of your regard, but you can't stay now

Mickey. And why the divil can't I?

Ninetta. Hush! don't talk so loud. I made a mistake. I thought there would be nobody here, but instead of that, there's a whole housefull of human combustibles, and I don't know when we may have an explosion.

Mickey. Being a sojir, you know, I'm used to them sort of playthings. Didn't I came over here from the blessed green island, and more betoken a deal greener I was than itself for that same. Didn't I pursue glory, as the recruiting-sargeant said, in coming here to help General Evans to powder the Carlists for Don Myjewel? and didn't we all get purty well powdered ourselves? and if I hadn't left off slaughtering the foe for slaughtering my fellow-creatures, in the shape of calves and sheep, it's lying peacably in the bed of glory I'd been long ago, with a daisy patthern quilt over me, to keep me from catching my death-cowld.

Ninetta. I tremble every moment you stay; go, now, or I shall be angry.

Mickey. Don't say that—I'm off. Give us one—just one, to keep the life in me till I see you again.

Ninetta. My gracious! my heart's in my mouth.

Mickey. Then it's all the closer to your lips, darling, and that improves the flavor wonderfully. [*kisses.*] Now I'm off, and indeed I have enough to do: this is one of my killing days!

Enter, at top, R. C., MANUEL.

I have a calf or two to despatch!

Ninetta. How coolly you talk of taking the lives of the poor innocents.

Mickey. Bless your tender little heart, it's nothing when you're used to it; a life's a life, you know, whatever dimensions it's in. You don't mind murdering a colony of spiders if they come in the way of business.

Ninetta. Don't talk so—don't. I couldn't kill anything for the world.

Mickey. Couldn't you, really. Did you ever eat an oyster?

Manuel. [*advancing.*] Silence, wretch!—Is this ruffian known to you?

Ninetta. Ruffian, indeed!

Manuel. Answer me at once.

Ninetta. Ye-yes, sir.

Manuel. And his dreadful trade.

Ninetta. Yes, sir.

Manuel. Away! Prepare to leave this house, immediately.

Ninetta. Gracious! the explosion's coming. Don't mind him, he's only jealous. I must find out Senor Leon before there's any mischief done. [*Exit,* R. C.

Manuel. Now, butcher, since that's your horrid trade, is it not?

Mickey. Why, yes, sir, just now, for the want of a better. Proud to serve you, sir, in any way.

Manuel. A heartless foreigner—the fittest for my purpose. How long have you followed this estimable calling?

Mickey. Well, not very long, your honor. You see, sir, this sort of killing is new to me: I've been a sojer.

Manuel. Oh! then, ,ou were early initiated into scenes of blood!

Mickey. Indeed, you may say that, sir, as far as shutting my two trigger eyes and firing away at random went.

Manuel. What a frightful patois!

Mickey. You may say it was a mighty frightful Pat-war! but there never was a war where the Pats was in, that they did not make it a little uncomfortable for some; for my own part, I fought as well as I could for the money I got, but, as good-luck would have it, I was killed at last.

Manuel. Killed!

Mickey. Yes, sir; at the close of a hard day's fight, I got shot in the throat by a quart-bottle, and was carried dead-drunk off the field, and when I came to my senses, I found I was condemned to be shot for mutinously knocking the head out of a whiskey barrel, so I took an opportunity, one fine day, to walk off with all the honors of war.

Manuel. Enough! my blood freezes to hear your coolness. Your present occupation pays you better, I presume.

Mickey. Why, to be sure it does. What I killed then, only went to the account of glory, but what I kill now turns into ready money.

Manuel. How so?

Mickey. How so? why don't I sell the carcases.

Manuel. What?

Mickey. And make a mighty pretty profit out of the skins.

Manuel. My friend, you set about your sanguinary business with true gusto, one would almost suppose you killed for pleasure.

Mickey. Not exactly. I kill for food: do you see the joke? Ha, ha!

Manuel. I know—I know; Hunger has goaded many a poor wretch to crime. Approach! nearer—don't laugh, it chills me to the heart to hear you.

Mickey. I can't help it, sir—upon my word I can't—it's constitutional.

Manuel. Cold-blooded miscreant! But to business; you know what you came here for?

Mickey. Know it—I should think so: to pierce the tender and susceptible heart of ——

Manuel. Silence!—I see you understand: let it be done.

Mickey. Don't be at all alarmed; I have a peculiar way of my own.

Manuel. You won't flinch?

Mickey. Is it me? Man alive, you don't know what I'm made of. Stop—let me see—a thought strikes me; you seem mighty anxious about this affair.

Manuel. Anxious! yes, I am anxious.

Mickey. Would it be a mighty great liberty if I was to ask you if you have a reason for getting rid of that same individual.

Manuel. Suffice it to say I have.

Mickey. A pretty noose you'd have me put my head into. It appears to me, sir, that if I understand you rightly, you want me to take off an individual that you have good reasons to wish removed.

Manuel. Speak lower. Decidedly you've just hit it, but assuredly not without a weighty consideration: here is a portion to begin. [*gives purse.*]

Mickey. A portion, a marriage portion.

Manuel. Just as you please, I care not what you do with it.

Mickey. Well, upon my soul, you're a purty sort of a chap, aint you!

Manuel. No recriminations—no compunctions. Will you do it, or shall I seek another mercenary wretch? You are silent—you consent 'Tis well. Is that the knife?

Mickey. What knife?

Manuel. The instrument of your detestable trade?

Mickey. Yes; tidy bit of stuff, aint it?

Manuel. It will do. Now all that remains for me to say is—that's the chamber.

Mickey. Oh, that's it, is it?

Manuel. Yes, and here's the key.

Mickey. Thank you.

Manuel. Hush! be expeditious—no noise, hush!

[*Exits mysteriously*, L. C.

Mickey. Well, if that ain't as mysterious a creature as ever puzzled a man of limited comprehension. I'll turn Turk, and live upon Russian ducks. He's either mad or drunk—not that there's much differ between the two. I wonder where my Ninetta has cut off to. I'll just bid her good-bye and start. What the devil did he mean by—Hush! no noise, that's the door? [*Imitating the other.*]

Enter hurriedly ANITA, R. C., *grasps* MICKEY.

Anita. Man of blood, desist.

Mickey. Hallo, what the devil's the matter now?

Anita. You know not what a crime you are about to commit.

Mickey. Upon my soul, you're right there.

Anita. You acknowledge it; indeed, indeed, it is a mistake.

Mickey. I should think it was.

Anita. I know it is.

Mickey. I'm rejoiced to hear it.

Anita. Give me that dreadful knife.

Mickey. I shan't do anything of the sort.

Anita. I implore you to surrender that instrument of death.

Mickey. What for, my good lady? I can't very well get on without it. This must be a mad-house, or I'm drunk and seeing visions, I don' know which.

Anita. Suffer me to take it from ou?

Mickey. I'd rather not give it up, if it's all the same to you. I must be gentle, or maybe I may set her raving. The fact is, my dear madam, I want it myself. I'm just going to make use of it.

Anita. [*Screams*] No, no; unsay those fearful words. Stay one moment—hear me! It is jealousy, false, groundless jealousy, which has driven him to take this desperate step.

Mickey. Is it, indeed, ma'm? Poor fellow. I wish I could cry a bit.

Anita. Yes, yes! and butcher though you are, I entreat you to pause before you shed innocent blood.

Mickey. I'd oblige you if I could, ma'm, but if you'll be good enough to recollect, I never shed anything else.

Anita. True, true; 'tis your abhorrent trade; and ye, methinks I see commiseration in your eye.

Mickey. Maybe you do, ma'm. I mustn't contradict her—she's as mad as a Millerite.

Anita. May I hope, then, that you relent?

Mickey. Indeed, ma'm, if it will do you any good, you may.

Anita. Bless you for that word—it has removed a mountain load from my heart.

Mickey. Has it, really? then I dare say you feel all the lighter. [ANITA *tries to take away knife.*] Ah! would you—they're mighty deceitful when they're in this state, I've heard.

Anita. Hark! 'tis his footstep.

Mickey. I wouldn't be surprised if it was.

Anita. It is!

Mickey. You're right, decidedly it is.

Anita. Hush! take this purse; only keep in your present mind, and its contents shall be doubled.

Mickey. Will it! You don't say so. Then with a blessing on the endeavor, I'll try to keep straight.

Anita. Will you swear it?

Mickey. Upon my soul.

Anita. Enough. I'll trust you. If he should question you, prevaricate.

Mickey. I will.

Anita Say—'tis done.

Mickey. 'Tis done.

Anita. He comes! remember. [*Exit*, L. 2 E.

Mickey. Remember! bedad, I'll never forget if I was to live to be as old as a couple of Methusalem's. I never saw a madder female since the day I left Molly Maguire, hurling benedictions after me at the cove of Cork. Let's see if its real money they've trusted her wid—why, I'll be hanged if it ain't. [*As he counts the money*

Enter MANUEL, L. C., *touches him on shoulder.*

Manuel. Well!

Mickey. How are you again, sir. Maybe this is the chap she was expecting. I'll try—Hush! it's *done!*

Manuel. Good! Ha! what's that? [*Snatches purse.*] Her purse, as I live; another damning evidence of her guilt.

Mickey. Come, I say, fair play's a jewel; that's mine.

Manuel. I know, wretch! your lawful spoil, torn from his prostrate body, was it not?

Mickey. Not a bit of it—I mean, yes. Damn it, this is another of them—there's a whole handful, and that little devil not to tell me a word about it.

Manuel. Hark! is he dead?

Enter LEON *at back*, R. C.

Mickey. Dead!

Manuel. Aye, dead?

Mickey. Dead as a herring.

Manuel. Then she shall follow. [*Exit*, L. C.

Mickey. With all my heart, and serve her quite right, I should say.

Leon. [*Seizes him by the throat.*] Bloodthirsty villain—vile remorseless wretch!

Mickey. Murder alive—they're all running about wild. It's the full of the moon!

Leon. Prepare to die, villain, although such consideration you do not deserve.

Mickey. Don't be a fool; what the devil are you about. Take it easy; what's it all about?

Leon. Have you not murdered him? speak.

Mickey. No, I believe not.

Leon. Liar!

Mickey. That is to say—wait a bit, let me think. Yes, I think I have. But wait, at this minute I give you my word I can't exactly remember.

Leon. Vile, prevaricating caitiff; did I not overhear you tell your fellow scoundrel, Manuel, that you had slain my brother.

Mickey. Was it your brother; did I do such an ungentlemanly thing; do give me time to consider!

Leon. Speak, or instant death awaits you!

Mickey. Well, then, I suppose I must have killed him.

Leon. Then follow thy victim. [*About to stab him.*]

Enter MANUEL, L. C.

Manuel. How now, young sir; would you tempt your villain brother's fate?

Leon. He was no villain.

Mickey. I most sincerely hope they'll humor one another if they're inclined to fight.

Leon. 'Tis you are the villain; hasty and remorseless, your unjust suspicions have urged you even to murder. My brother was innocent of any wrong to thee.

Manuel. No, no! I could not have been deceived—he betrayed me and has perished for it.

Leon. 'Tis false as thine own false heart.

Isabel. [*Without*, L. 2 E.] Where is he—where is the assassin of my love?

Mickey. Holy St. Donnybrook, here comes another! Where the devil's the keepers?

Manuel. That voice—who spoke?

Leon. Your wife's sister, Isabella; the betrothed of him whom you have so foully butchered!

Manuel. No, no! it cannot be.

Enter ISABELLA, L. 2 E.

Isabel. Cruel, cruel, heartless man, to take a life that was so dear to me!

Mickey. They're all in a story; I wish I could get out.

Isabel. How has your fatal jealousy blinded your reason! It was to me that those attentions were addressed which you thought were bestowed upon your wife—to me, whose life, and love, and happiness, were all centered in him, and now my heart is widowed by a brother's hand.

Manuel. Oh, fool! fool! thoughtless, blind, inhuman villain!

Mickey. It's getting rather serious. [*Stealing out.*]

Manuel. Where is that cool, heartless witness of my villany? Ha, think not to skulk away;—had not thy ready knife been anxious for the horrid deed, it might now have been undone.

Isabel. Is this the fiend?

Leon. Hold no longer parley with the assassin, but let us each kill our share of him. Die, villain! [MANUEL *and* LEON *rush at him.*]

Andrea. [*From chamber.*] Hold! [*They pause.*]

Isabel. That voice! 'tis Andrea's!—alive!

Manuel. What juggle is this—the key?

Mickey. What key? Oh, aye—here you are.

[MANUEL *opens door.*—ANDREA *embraces* ISABELLA. *Enter* ANITA, *who embraces* MANUEL. MICKEY *embraces* LEON.

Mickey. By the powers I'm mighty glad there's a lucid interval.

Manuel. My dear true-hearted wife, how nearly did my groundless jealousy cause me to commit a deed which would have embittered my after life: say but that I am forgiven, and the shadow of a doubt shall never cross me more.

Anita. Ah, Manuel, you know how zealous a counsellor you have in my unchanged affection. Jealousy, the offspring of o'er anxious love, leaves no ill-feeling in a woman's heart: there is my hand.

Manuel. Of you and all, I have to ask most humble pardon; but for this murderer, here ——

Mickey. Hallo! the moon's rising again. You'll pardon me, sir, but as you seem to have come slightly to your little bit of original sense, let me inform you that it was love, and not murder, that brought me here.

Manuel. Indeed!

Ninetta. I'll answer for that, sir, such as it is. What! my intended murder? Yes, as far as a good fat sheep goes, I grant you.

Nickey. Yes, and that's justifiable homicide, all the world over.

Manuel. Thank fortune, then, which threw you in my way, and pray forgive me, my fine fellow, for so greatly mistaking your useful vocation.

Isabel
Anita, &c. } And me. [*shake hands.*

Mickey. Don't mention it. I'm not exactly sure if their wits are in the right place yet: I'll see. You recollect giving me this bit of money to take care of for you, when you were raving. I mean ——

Anita. Keep it—it is the least I can do to atone for my unjust estimate of your character.

Manuel. I shall add something to it, also.

All. And so shall I, and I, &c.

Mickey. I'm satisfied. The verdict of the jury is, sensible all round. Long life to you all, and that you may never think of a worse way to get rid of your small change; and now, if my darling Ninetta will ac cept this hand, red with the blood of beef and mutton, why I'll cut the slaughterer's trade, take a bit of garden ground, and go into the nursery business.

Ninetta. It would be cowardly to shrink now; there, I have no fears of your killing me!

Mickey. If I do, it will be with kindness, you bewildering little divil of an angel. I'm so nearly happy, there's only one thing remains to make me completely so; and that is, that you, who are a whole court of justice, judges, jury, and witnesses, may look upon this case as merely a laughing matter. They say that the man who pleads his own cause, has a fool for a client, and, indeed, if there was a counsellor here would volunteer in my defence, I really wouldn't say a word; but in my present situation, what am I to do? You are called upon to decide upon the merits of this case; and as you are your own witnesses, why you'll escape a jolly lot of balleyragging, and return a verdict according to the evidence. Now, I contend, that there is not a particle of evidence that can convict me of even an attempt to kill anything but Time: if I have succeeded in that, I feel that your sense of justice will cause you to return a verdict in my favor, without leaving your boxes.

THE END.

www.ingramcontent.com/pod-product-compliance
Lightning Source LLC
LaVergne TN
LVHW011147110826
845150LV00008B/2562

* 9 7 8 1 4 1 8 1 9 1 6 7 2 *